Fun to Trace

Cover illustrated by Lindsey Sarles McCool
Illustrated by Martha Avilés, Tiphanie Beeke, Michelle Berg, and Peggy Tagel

Louis Weber, C.E.O.
Publications International, Ltd.
7373 North Cicero Avenue
Lincolnwood, Illinois 60712
Ground Floor, 59 Gloucester Place
London W1U 8JJ

Customer Service: 1-800-595-8484 or customer_service@pilbooks.com

www.pilbooks.com

p i kids is a registered trademark of Publications International, Ltd.

8 7 6 5 4 3 2 1

Manufactured in China.

ISBN-13: 978-1-60553-648-4
ISBN-10: 1-60553-648-2

D1358660

Welcome!

This Fun to Trace workbook has been specially designed to help prepare your child for school. You and your child should work together on each activity. In the front of the book, you will find simple, introductory exercises. As you work your way to the back of the book, the exercises will gradually become more complex and challenging.

Before you begin, show your child how to hold a marker properly. Your child should pinch the marker between the thumb and index finger. The side of the marker should rest against the side of the middle finger. As your child practices tracing this way, they will build important fine motor skills. As children gain fine motor skills, they build strength in the small muscles in their hands. Activities that require fine motor skills, such as coloring and tracing, develop the accuracy and control children need in order to learn

to write. Building these important skills helps prepare your child for school.

In addition to developing fine motor skills, the exercises in this book will challenge your child to distinguish shapes, practice counting, and follow simple directions. To make the most of each activity, keep these suggestions in mind:

• Tear out the page along the perforation and lay it flat on your work surface. This will help your child focus on just one activity at a time.

• Read the directions aloud.

• Let your child attempt each activity and only assist when necessary.

• Be positive and encouraging. Learning should be fun!

When you reach the end of the workbook, celebrate your child's accomplishments. Remove the certificate of achievement and help your child write their name on it so they can proudly display it.

Certificate of Achievement

I can TRACE!

Congratulations!

Taylor
(name)

has successfully completed the FUN TO TRACE workbook

Presented on December 23rd

Presented by Mom

Straight Lines

Follow the paths.

 Start on the green dot and stop on the red dot.

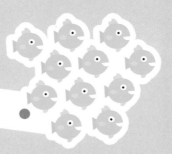

Straight Lines

Follow the paths.

Curves

Follow the paths.

Curves
Follow the paths.

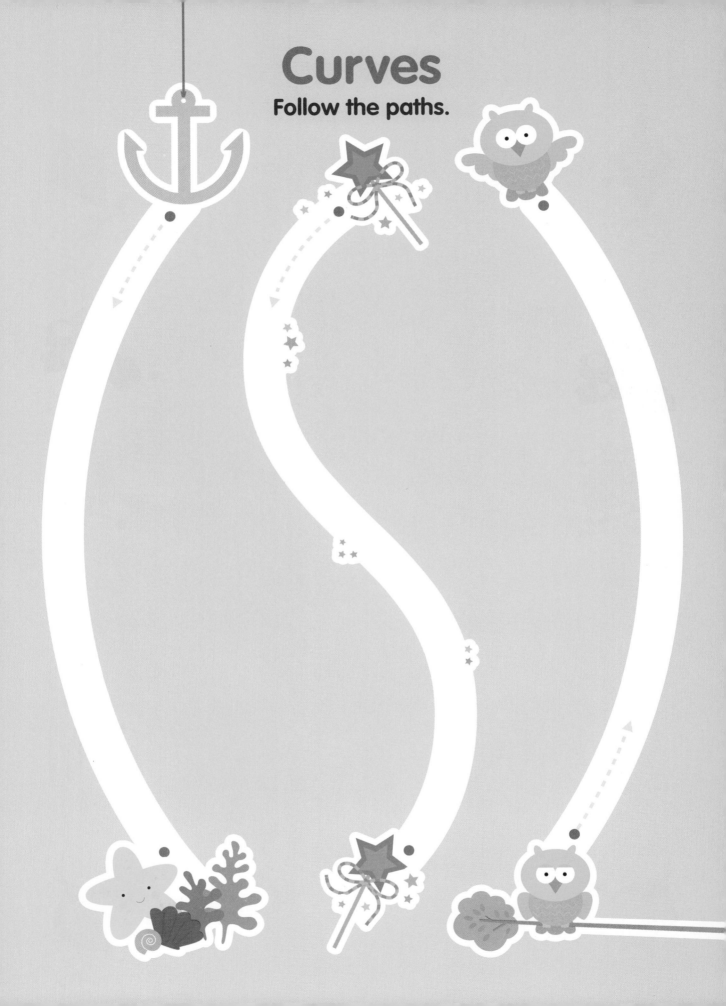

Zigzags

Follow the paths.

Zigzags

Follow the paths.

Loops

Follow the paths.

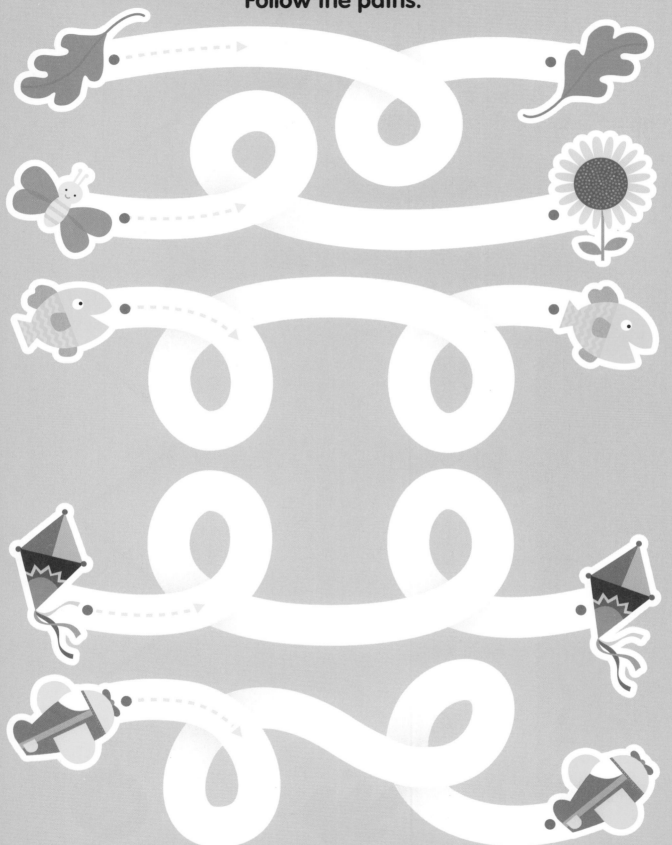

Loops

Follow the paths.

Straight Lines and Curves

Show off your skills!

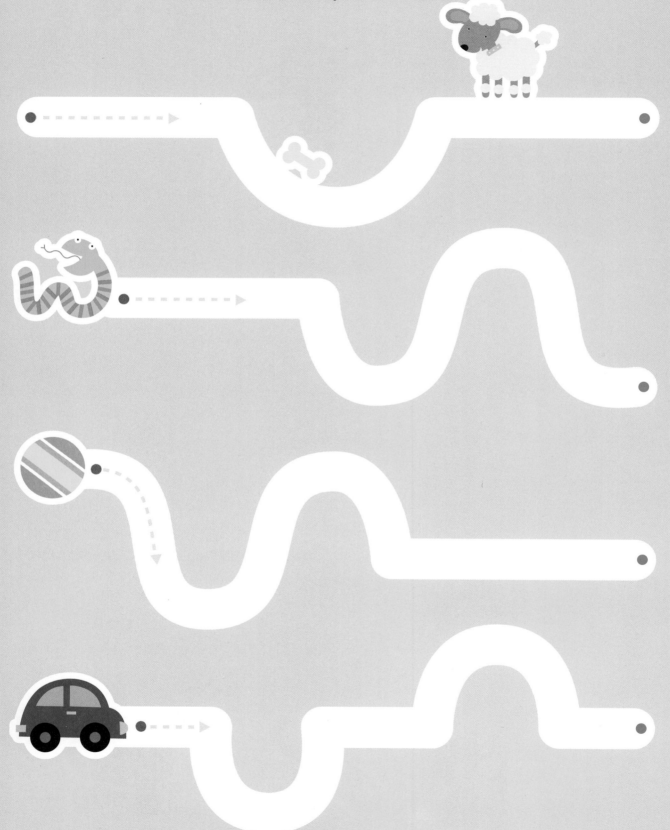

Zigzags and Loops

Show off your skills!

Circle

Trace the shapes.

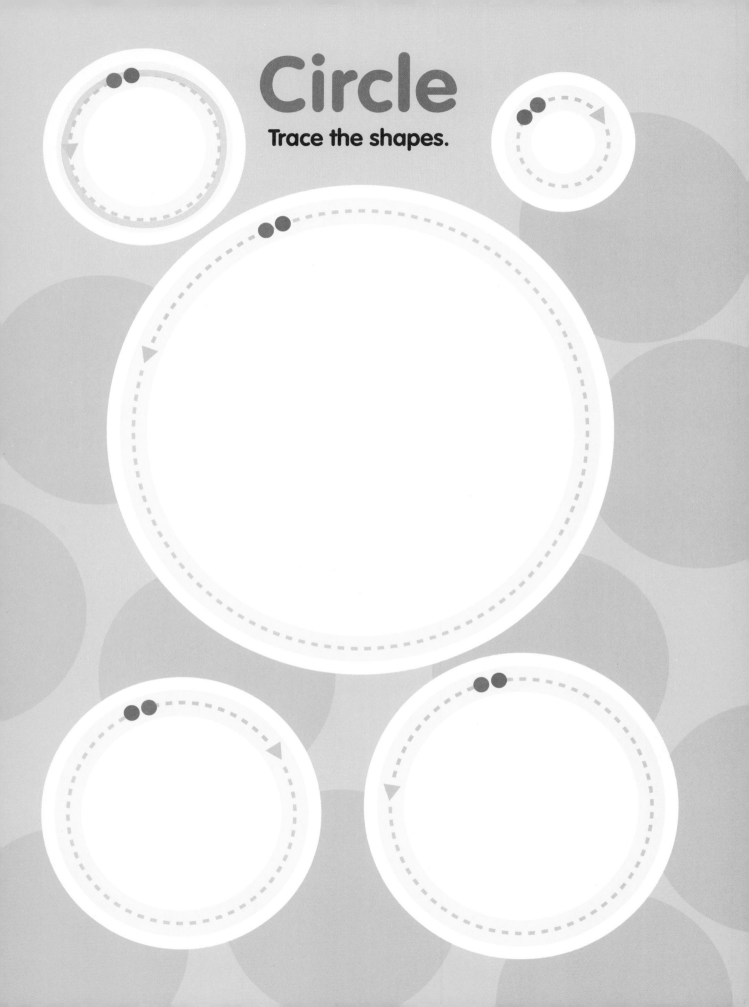

Circle

Trace the shapes.

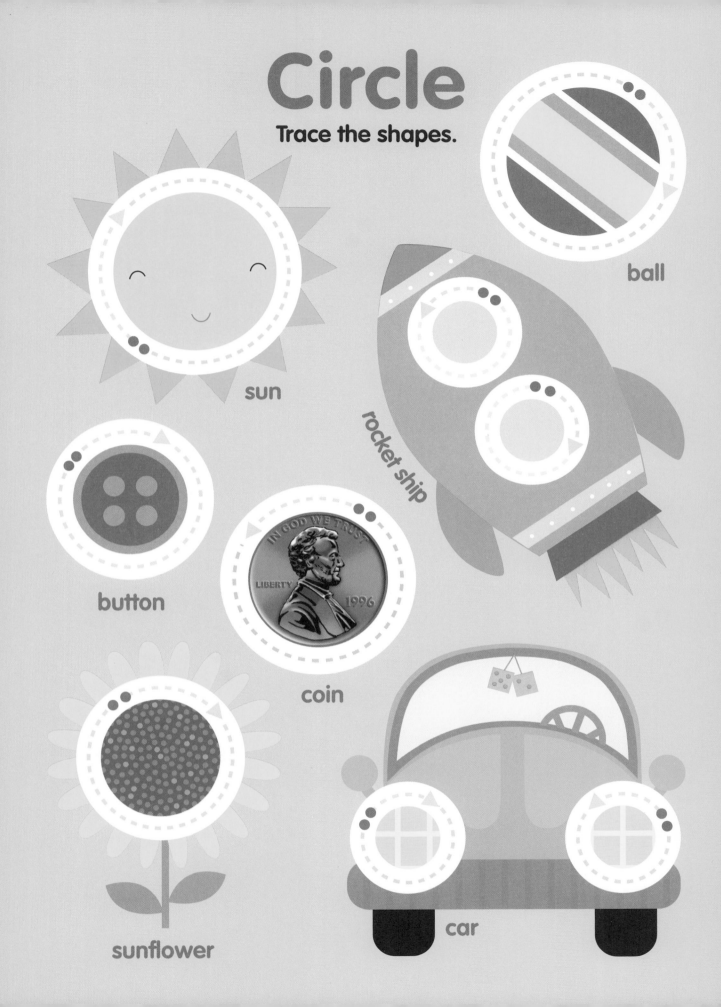

ball

sun

rocket ship

button

coin

sunflower

car

Triangle

Trace the shapes.

Triangle

Trace the shapes.

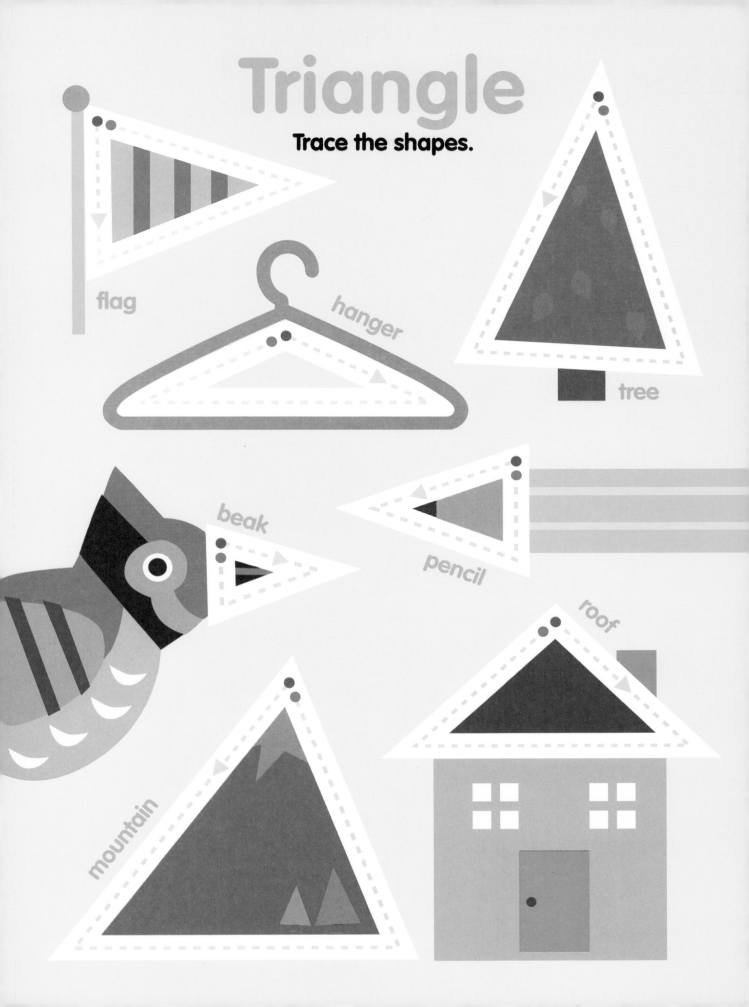

flag

hanger

tree

beak

pencil

roof

mountain

Square

Trace the shapes.

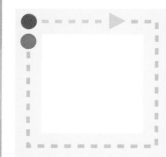

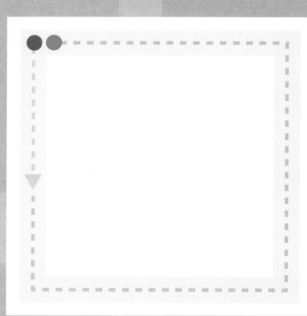

Square

Trace the shapes.

fish tank

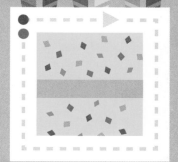

cake

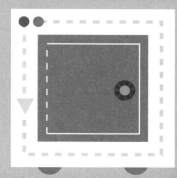

safe

blocks

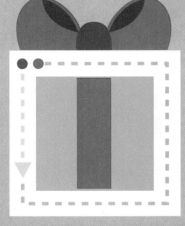

house

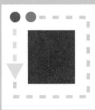

school bus

gift

Rectangle

Trace the shapes.

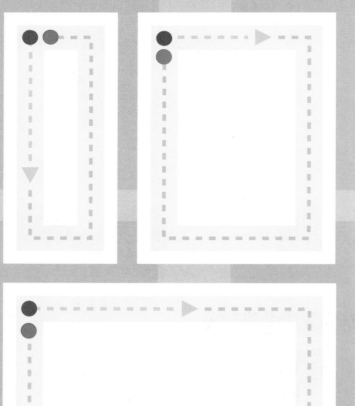

Rectangle

Trace the shapes.

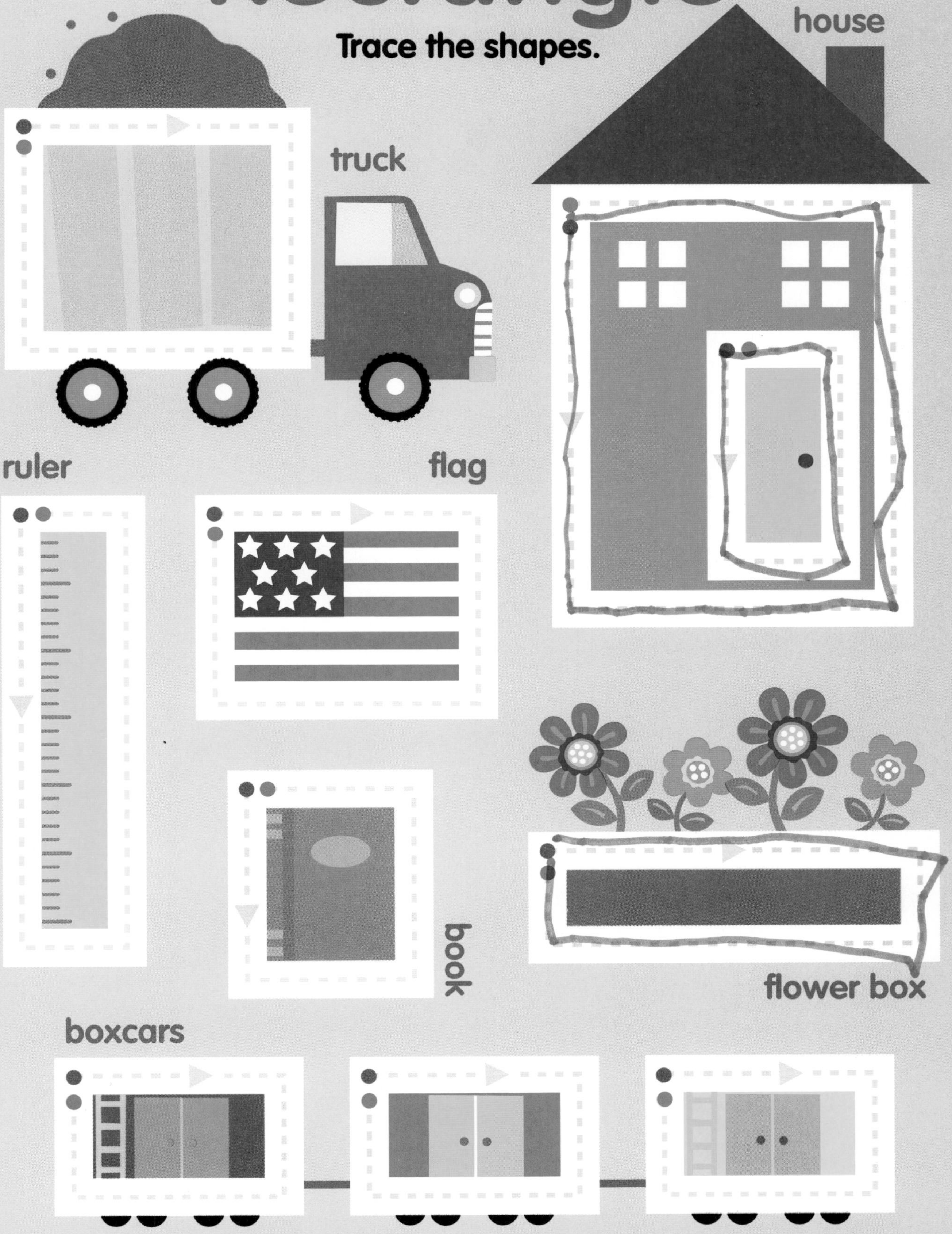

house

truck

ruler

flag

book

flower box

boxcars

Diamond

Trace the shapes.

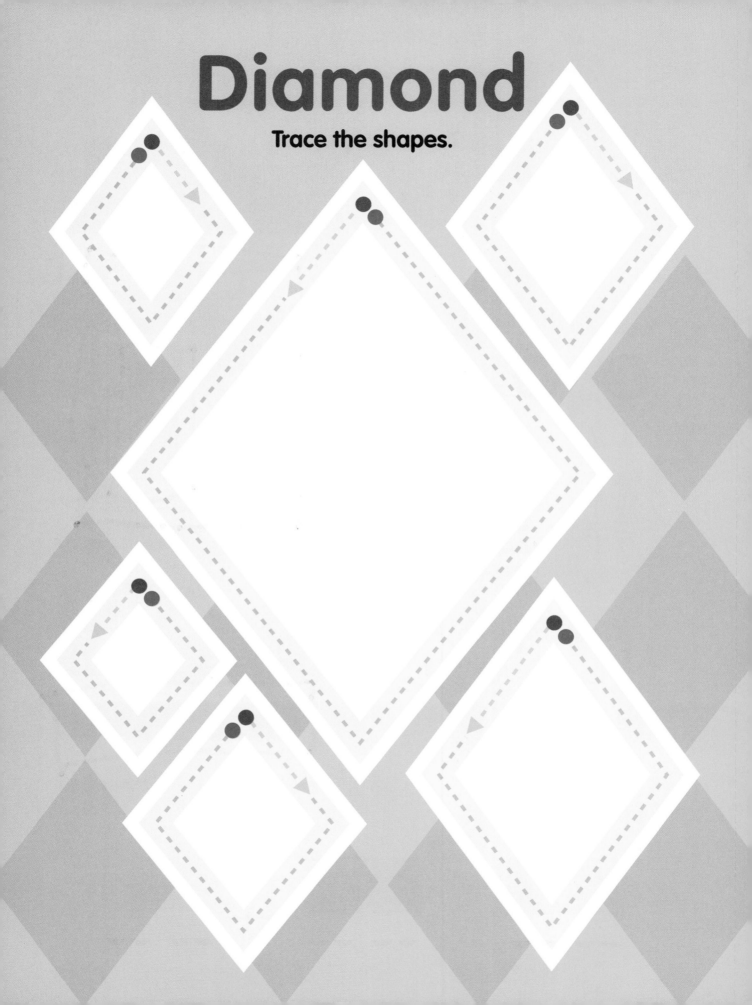

Diamond

Trace the shapes.

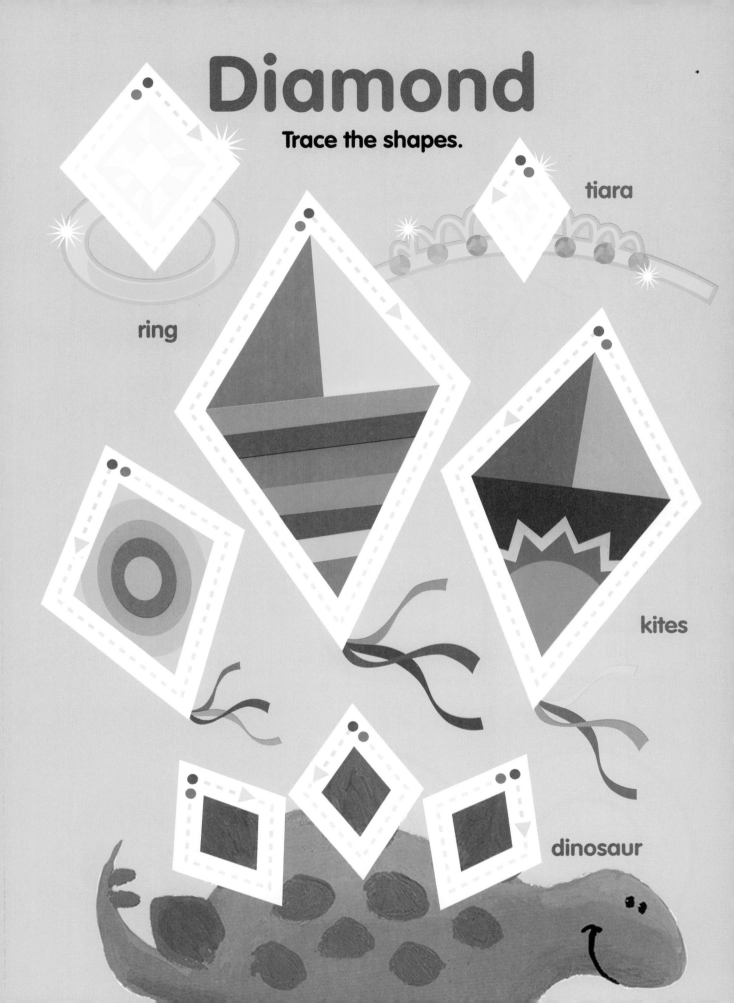

ring

tiara

kites

dinosaur

Alphabet

Trace the letters.

apple

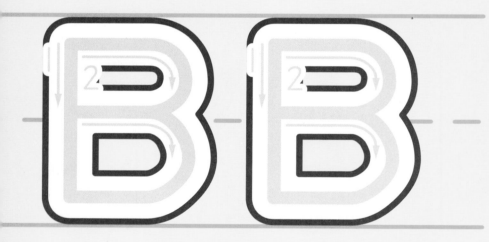

butterfly

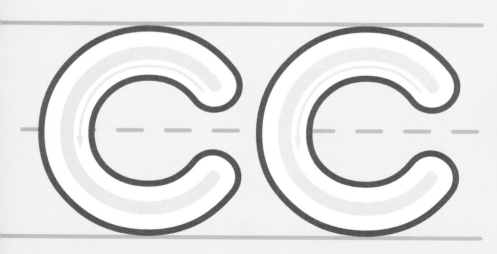

car

Alphabet

Keep tracing!

Alphabet

Trace the letters.

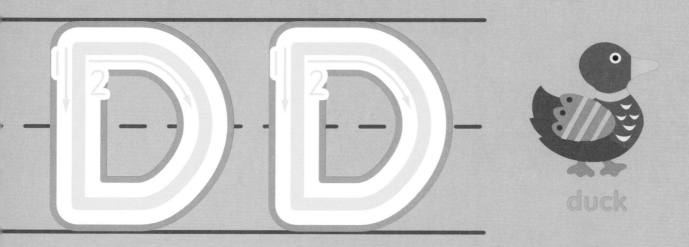

duck

elephant

flower

Alphabet

Keep tracing!

Alphabet

Trace the letters.

guitar

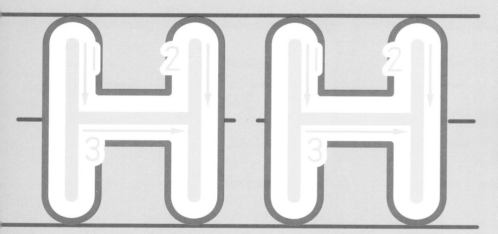

helicopter

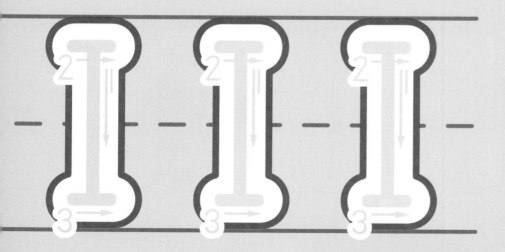

ice cream

Alphabet

Keep tracing!

G G G G

H H H H H

I I I I I

Alphabet

Trace the letters.

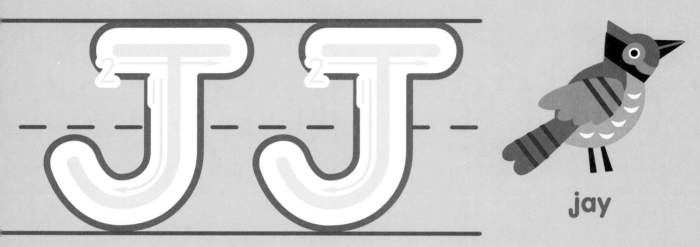

jay

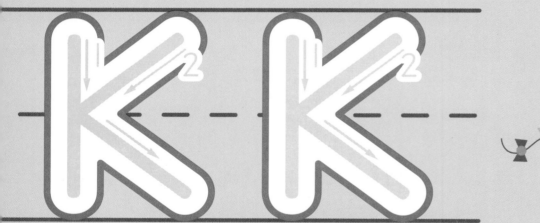

kite

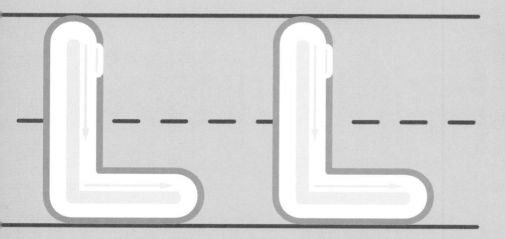

lion

Alphabet

Keep tracing!

J J J J

K K K K

L L L L

Alphabet

Trace the letters.

monkey

nest

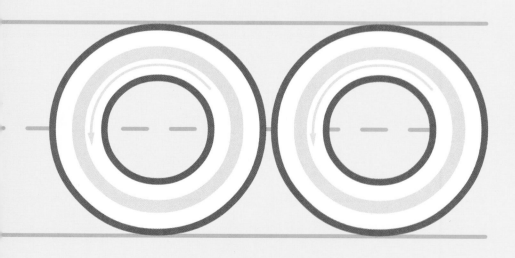

owl

Alphabet

Keep tracing!

M M M

N N N N

O O O

Alphabet

Trace the letters.

pear

quail

rabbit

Alphabet

Keep tracing!

Alphabet

Trace the letters.

sailboat

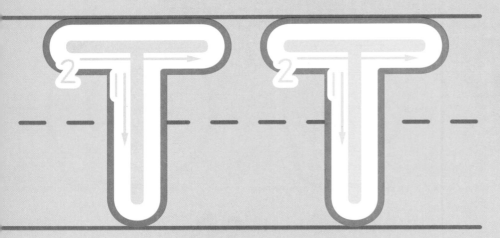

turtle

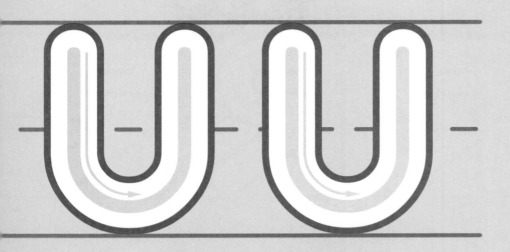

umbrella

Alphabet

Keep tracing!

S S S S

T T T T

U U U U

Alphabet

Trace the letters.

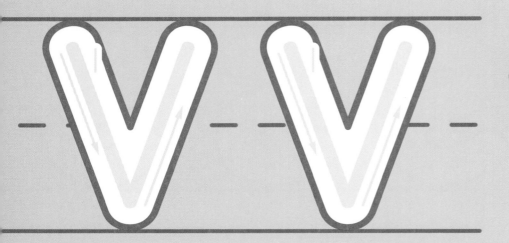

valentine

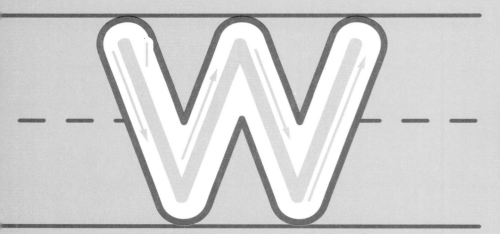

walrus

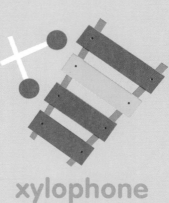

xylophone

Alphabet

Keep tracing!

V V V V

W W W W

X X X X

Alphabet

Trace the letters.

yo-yo

zebra

Yay! I did it!

Alphabet

Keep tracing!

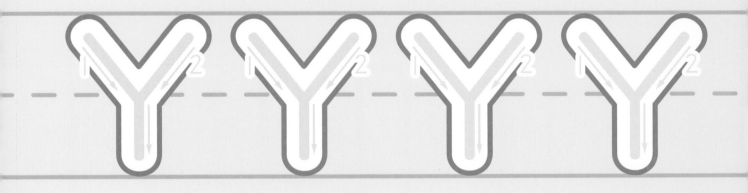

Y Y Y Y

Z Z Z Z

Now I know my ABC's!

Numbers

Trace the numbers.

How many school buses are on this page?
Try tracing the school bus.

school bus

Numbers

Keep tracing!

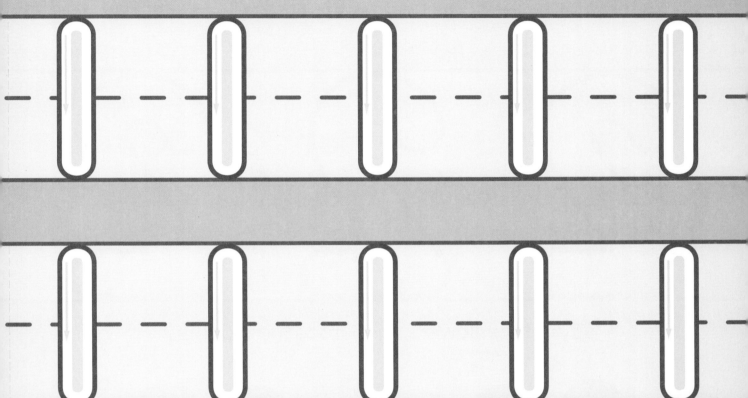

Circle one apple:

Circle one butterfly:

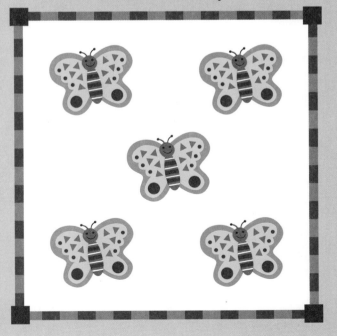

Numbers

Trace the numbers.

2 2 2

Count the flowers, then trace the blooms.

Numbers

Keep tracing!

Circle two cars:

Circle two ducks:

Numbers

Trace the numbers.

Count the kites, then trace the wind that carries them.

Numbers

Keep tracing!

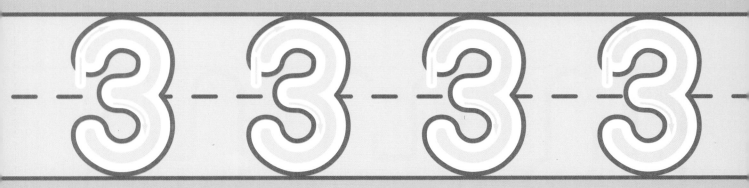

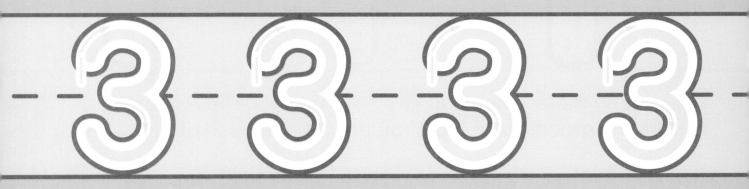

Circle three elephants:

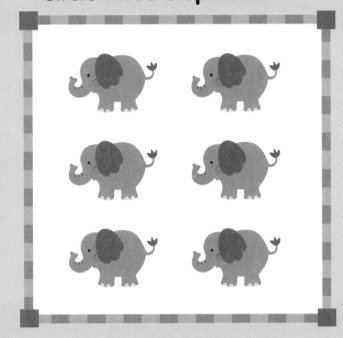

Circle three flowers:

Numbers

Trace the numbers.

How many clouds do you see? Can you draw a line from the green dot to the airplane without touching a cloud?

Numbers

Keep tracing!

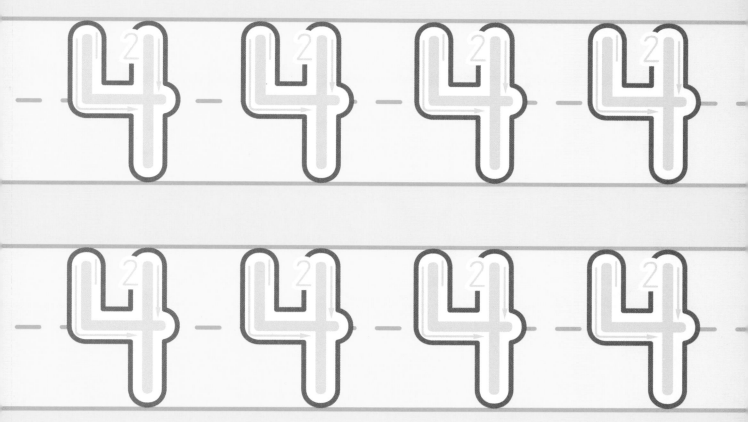

Circle four guitars:

Numbers

Trace the numbers.

5 5 5

Draw a line from the green dot to the red dot through all five tops. Count them as you go!

Numbers

Keep tracing!

Circle five helicopters:

Numbers

Trace the numbers.

6 6 6

Count the boxcars, then draw a line
to link them all together.

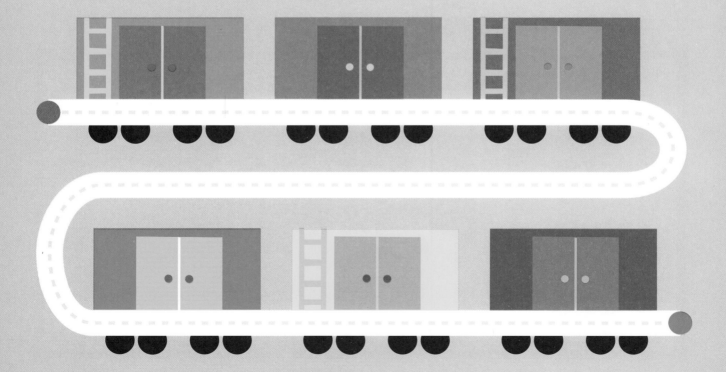

Numbers

Keep tracing!

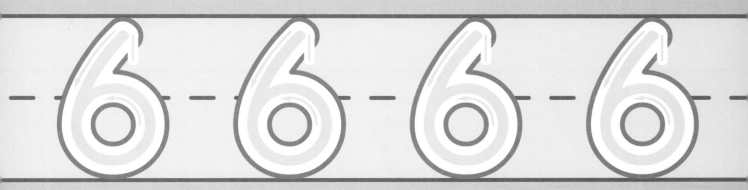

Circle six blue jays:

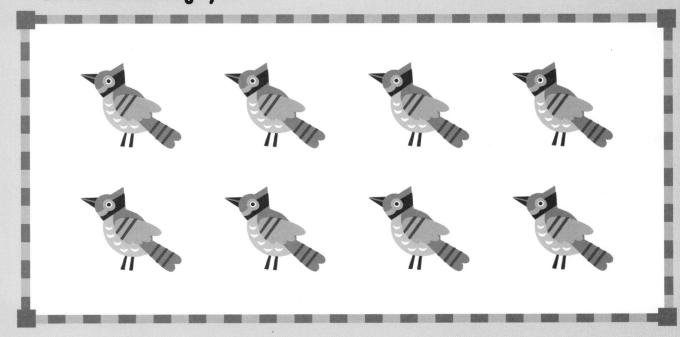

Numbers

Trace the numbers.

7 7 7

How many frogs can you count?
Try tracing a curvy path through the group.

Numbers

Keep tracing!

Circle seven lions:

Numbers

Trace the numbers.

How many turtles can you count?
Draw a line through the turtles from smallest to largest.

Numbers

Keep tracing!

Circle eight pears:

Numbers

Trace the numbers.

Can you draw a line from the green dot to the red dot without touching any of the cakes? Count them as you go!

Numbers

Keep tracing!

9 9 9 9

9 9 9 9

Circle nine rabbits:

Numbers

Trace the numbers.

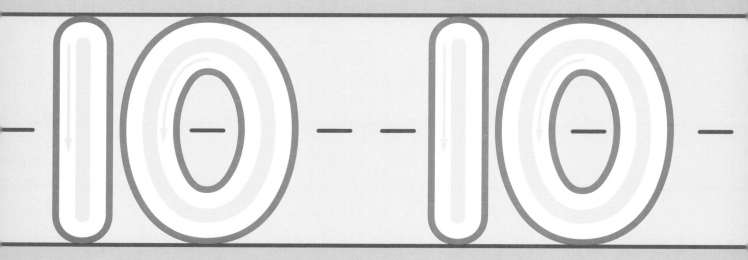

Practice tracing 1 to 5 as you count these tasty cones.

Numbers

Keep tracing!

10 10 10

10 10 10

Now practice tracing 6 to 10!

  6  7   8

  9    10

Whale

Trace the whale's waterspout and the wave.

Octopus

Trace the octopus's arms.

Crab

Trace the crab.

Turtle

Trace the turtle as he swims.

Fish

Trace the fish and the shiny pearl.

Jellyfish

Trace the squiggly jellyfish tentacles.

Shoes

Trace the swirly laces.

Mittens

Trace the bear and his warm mittens.

Glasses

Trace these fun frames.

Hat

Trace the bear's fancy feathered cap.

Princess

Trace her dress and her twinkling tiara.

Castle

Trace the place where the princess lives.

Train

Trace the train as it travels.

Dump Truck

Trace the truck as it climbs.

Submarine

Trace this sunken sub.

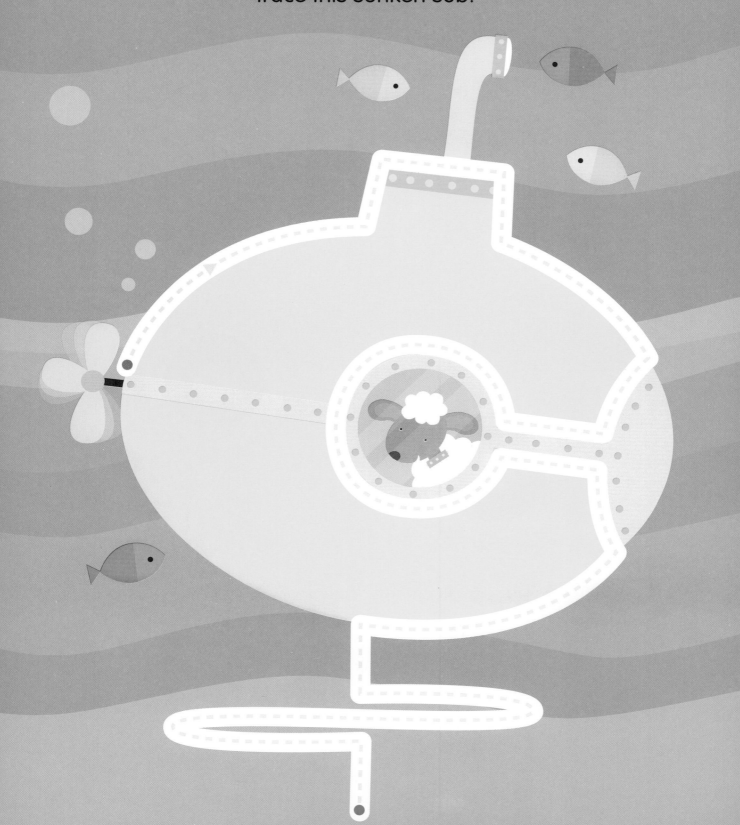

Rocket

Zoom! Trace the rocket out in space.

Car

Beep! Beep! Trace the car.

Hot-Air Balloon

Trace the hot-air balloon rising up, up, up!

Poodle

Poodle was playing and lost her toy. Can you help?

Sea Horse

Sea Horse is doing a starfish dance. Let's follow along!

Snake

Help the snake travel through the yard
without touching any flowers.

Hopscotch

Can you hop your way through?

Tiger

Follow the playful tiger's path.

Monkey

Can you help the monkey collect all the bananas on the way to the forest? Draw a line through each of the bananas as you pick it up!

Giraffe

Can you connect all the spots and dots?

Elephant

Trace the momma elephant's path as she looks for her babies.

Zebra & Hippo

Zebra is planning to visit his friend, Hippo.
Can you help him find his way?

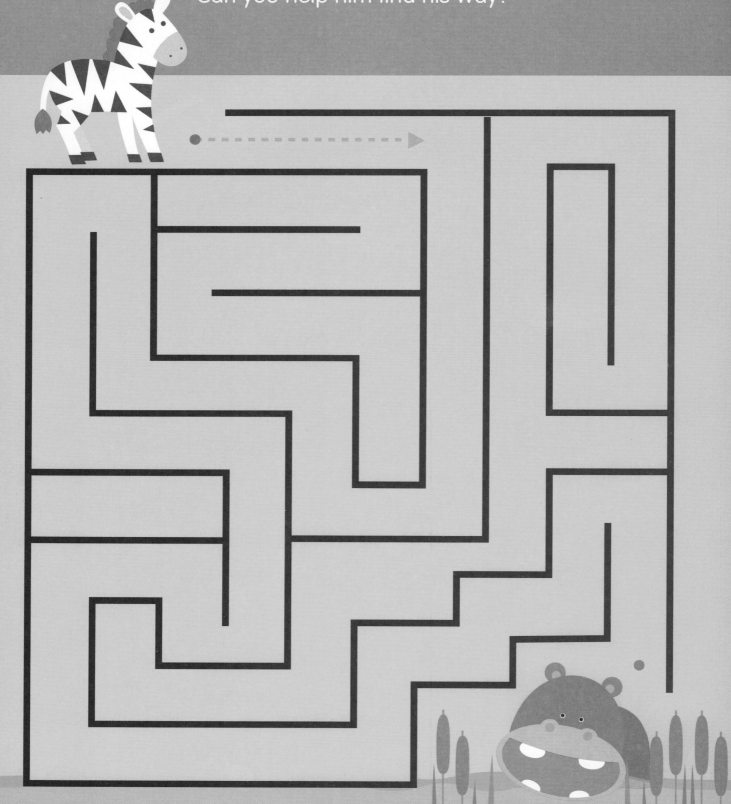

Wild Animals

This pilot wants to photograph wild animals.
Can you help him find some?

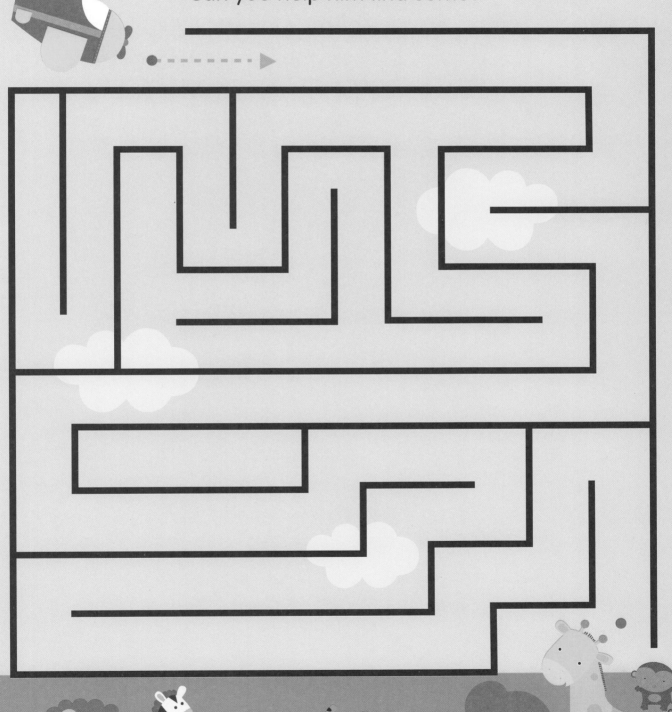

Lion

Little Lion is lost. Can you help him find his way to the jungle?

Owl

Can you help Owl fly high, high up to the moon?

Pear

Complete the maze, then color in the path.

Sailboat

Complete the maze, then color in the path.

You're a Star!

Complete the maze, then color in the path.

Certificate of Achievement

I can TRACE!

Congratulations!

_____
(name)

has successfully completed the FUN TO TRACE workbook.

Presented on _____

Presented by _____

Certificate of Achievement

I learned a lot!

☐ I practiced tracing on paths.

☐ I traced the alphabet A to Z.

☐ I traced the numbers 1 to 10.

☐ I completed mazes.

☐ I followed directions.

☐ I can trace anything!